LOVELAND PUBLIC LIBRARY

000522790

Withdrawn

D0824424

THAT ROCKS!

WEATHERING AND EROSION

By Maria Nelson

Gareth Stevens
Publishing

Please visit our website, www.garethstevens.com. For a free color catalog of all our high-quality books, call toll free 1-800-542-2595 or fax 1-877-542-2596.

Library of Congress Cataloging-in-Publication Data

Nelson, Maria.
  Weathering and erosion / Maria Nelson.
      p. cm. — (That rocks!)
  Includes index.
  ISBN 978-1-4339-8330-6 (pbk.)
  ISBN 978-1-4339-8331-3 (6-pack)
  ISBN 978-1-4339-8329-0 (library binding)
  1. Rocks—Juvenile literature. 2. Erosion—Juvenile literature. I. Title.
  QE432.2.N44 2014
  551.3'02—dc23
                                    2012047239

First Edition

Published in 2014 by
Gareth Stevens Publishing
111 East 14th Street, Suite 349
New York, NY 10003

Copyright © 2014 Gareth Stevens Publishing

Designer: Katelyn Londino
Editor: Kristen Rajczak

Photo credits: Cover, p. 1 ian woolcock/Shutterstock.com; p. 5 leospek/Shutterstock.com; p. 7 Stanislav Komogorov/Shutterstock.com; pp. 9, 13 iStockphoto/Thinkstock.com; p. 11 Oliver Strewe/Lonely Planet Images/Getty Images; p. 15 Berthold Trenkel/Photosdisc/Getty Images; p. 17 © iStockphoto.com/BIHAIBO; p. 19 David P. Lewis/Shutterstock.com; p. 20 (inset) Franois De Heel/Garden Picture Library/Getty Images.

All rights reserved. No part of this book may be reproduced in any form without permission in writing from the publisher, except by a reviewer.

Printed in the United States of America

CPSIA compliance information: Batch #CS13GS: For further information contact Gareth Stevens, New York, New York at 1-800-542-2595.

CONTENTS

Words in the glossary appear in **bold** type the first time they are used in the text.

HAPPENING EVERYWHERE

Loveland Public Library
Loveland, CO

Have you ever seen a tree's roots breaking through the sidewalk in your neighborhood? Or maybe you've seen a gust of wind pick up dry soil and toss it in the air when it hasn't rained for a while. Both of these can be examples of weathering and erosion where you live!

The results of weathering and erosion may be more extraordinary, too. From the Grand Canyon to the cliffs of Iceland, these important **processes** can change the shape of Earth.

Travelers in Iceland can stand far above the ocean on cliffs formed by weathering and erosion.

WHAT'S WEATHERING?

Though they often work together, weathering and erosion are different processes. Weathering is the breakdown of rock into **sediment**.

Physical weathering is one way rock may break down. Sometimes called mechanical weathering, physical weathering changes a rock's size or shape. This can happen when water flows into open spaces in the rock, freezes, and causes the rock to crack. Or, wind may blow matter at a rock and chip away little bits of it.

SET IN STONE

Rock expands in hot weather and shrinks in cold weather. Moving from one temperature extreme to another can cause rock to weaken and break more easily.

Physical weathering can cause stones to become smooth.

CONTINUING THE BREAKDOWN

Rocks are made of **minerals**. Adding new minerals, **chemicals**, or gases to a rock may change its makeup and cause it to break down. This is known as chemical weathering. Rain is a common way chemical weathering happens. Rainwater mixes with chemicals and minerals as it falls. It then flows over and into rocks.

Biological weathering is the breakdown of rock because of the actions of living things. Animals may dig through soft rock. Some **bacteria** make chemicals that break down rock, too.

SET IN STONE

How and when weathering occurs depends on a rock's mineral makeup, how fine or coarse its grains are, and the climate, or average weather of an area.

Mosses can cause biological weathering as they grow on the surface and into cracks of rocks.

EXPLAINING EROSION

After weathering creates sediment, the tiny bits of rock may stay where they are. However, sediment is often **transported** to another place. When sediment is moved away from where it was created and **deposited** in a new place, it's called erosion.

There are many natural **agents** of erosion. Gravity, or the force that pulls everything toward Earth's center, is one major agent of erosion. It may work by itself or with other agents to cause erosion in different places.

Depending on the conditions, gravity can cause erosion to occur slowly or quickly.

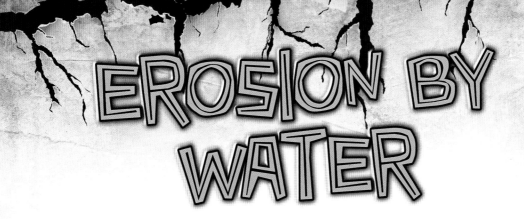

EROSION BY WATER

Water is as important in erosion as it is in weathering. It both breaks down rock into sediment and then carries it away. This can happen in any body of water. For example, waves beat against lake and ocean shores, pulling bits of existing rock out into the water. Rivers wear away their banks over time, too.

Rain causes erosion as well. Puddles form and begin to flow downhill, carrying soil and other matter. If enough rain falls to cause flooding, even more erosion occurs!

SET IN STONE

Since bodies of water play such a big part in erosion, lakes, rivers, and oceans have lots of sediment on their bottom!

Have you ever been at the beach when the **tide** comes in?
You might notice shells and rocks being deposited in the sand.
That's erosion in action!

13

WIND AND ICE

Wind is another agent of erosion. It blows around loose sand, soil, and other sediment. This often happens in very dry places, such as deserts. As wind moves some sediment, it creates even more sediment! Mountains and other landforms might be "sandblasted," or weathered by sand that's being transported by wind erosion.

Did you know glaciers cause erosion, too? Glaciers are huge, slow-moving slabs of ice. They loosen and move rocks. They also drag sediment along as they move.

SET IN STONE

People try to decrease erosion in dry areas by growing trees and plants to help hold the soil in place.

Glaciers melt and refreeze as they move.
This can cause weathering and erosion, too.

WORKING TOGETHER

Why do weathering and erosion happen? These Earth processes are steps in the rock cycle, a scientific model that explains how rock breaks down and re-forms over time. A group of rocks called sedimentary rocks are created from the sediment that's made by weathering and transported by erosion.

As steps in the rock cycle, weathering and erosion are part of the creation of almost all the rocks on Earth! Even rocks that form deep underground reach Earth's surface in time.

SET IN STONE

Sedimentary rock forms when sediment is buried under **pressure** and binds together. It then may be forced deeper underground to become the other types of rock—metamorphic rock and igneous rock.

Sometimes the terms "weathering" and "erosion" are used to mean the same thing. Remember, if sediment doesn't move, the process is weathering. If the sediment is transported and deposited, the process is erosion.

HARMFUL EROSION

Weathering and erosion are important to the formation of the rock on Earth. However, they can also be harmful and dangerous. Erosion can hurt a farmer's crops. In dry years, wind blows away needed topsoil. Heavy rainfall washes it away from plants that need it.

Rock loosened by weathering causes landslides and rock slides, fast-moving forms of erosion by gravity. These can fall on homes and block roads. When bad rainstorms occur, clay and soil can cause mudslides, too.

These signs let people know they're in a place
where rock slides are common.

KEEPING EROSION IN CHECK

Human actions can speed up erosion that harms our daily lives. Clearing large areas for buildings can cause soil erosion that might get into drinking water. And more erosion can increase the amount of dust carried by wind. This can spread illnesses!

However, careful planning can help slow erosion, even in your own backyard. Rain gardens, for example, are a beautiful way to collect and clean extra rainwater! Some have drains under them. Others have special plants growing in them that can withstand lots of water.

rain garden

THE PROCESS OF WEATHERING AND EROSION

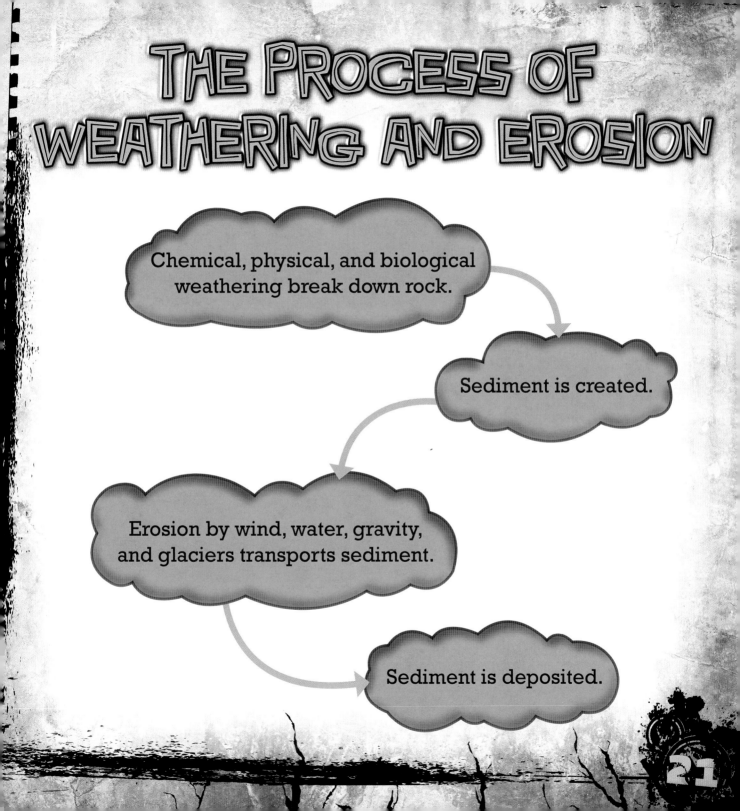

Chemical, physical, and biological weathering break down rock.

Sediment is created.

Erosion by wind, water, gravity, and glaciers transports sediment.

Sediment is deposited.

GLOSSARY

agent: something that produces an effect

bacteria: tiny creatures that can only be seen with a microscope

chemical: having to do with matter that can be mixed with other matter to cause changes. Also, the matter itself.

deposit: to let fall or sink

mineral: matter in the ground that forms rocks

physical: having to do with matter

pressure: the application of force

process: the set of steps that move something forward

sediment: matter, such as stones and sand, that is carried onto land or into the water by wind, water, or land movement

tide: the rising and falling of the surface of the ocean that happens twice a day

transport: to move people or things from one place to another

FOR MORE INFORMATION

Books

Kalman, Bobbie. *What Shapes the Land?* New York, NY: Crabtree Publishing, 2009.

Miller-Schroeder, Patricia. *The Rock Cycle.* New York, NY: AV2 by Weigl, 2011.

Websites

Photo Gallery: Erosion and Weathering
science.nationalgeographic.com/science/photos/weathering-erosion-gallery/
Check out examples of weathering and erosion in pictures from all over the world.

Rocky's Journey Around the Rock Cycle
www.oum.ox.ac.uk/thezone/rocks/cycle/index.htm
Use an interactive graphic of the rock cycle to learn more about this process.

Publisher's note to educators and parents: Our editors have carefully reviewed these websites to ensure that they are suitable for students. Many websites change frequently, however, and we cannot guarantee that a site's future contents will continue to meet our high standards of quality and educational value. Be advised that students should be closely supervised whenever they access the Internet.

INDEX